Creating Artwork For Book Covers

The Definitive Guide Using PowerPoint™

S.T. Mastroianni

"If I had an hour to solve a problem I'd spend 55 minutes thinking about the problem and 5 minutes thinking about solutions."

"The formulation of a problem is often more essential than its solution, which may be merely a matter of mathematical or experimental skills."

Albert Einstein

Contents

Preface

This book is aimed at authors that want to self-publish on Amazon or similar platforms without spending any money.

CreateSpace, a member of the Amazon group of companies, is used for publishing printed books.

Kindle Direct Publishing, KDP, is Amazon's electronic book distribution arm.

The purpose of this book is to provide a comprehensive set of instructions to produce the composite book cover artwork that meets or exceeds the minimum standards required by publishers.

CreateSpace was used as the target publisher during the entire process described because in this author's view it is the best provider of a low cost, or no cost, self publishing service.

Although CreateSpace will be referenced extensively, the final cover art will be exported in a format that is acceptable to many other publishers. The output of the work is therefore not limited exclusively to Amazon's CreateSpace.

There are no charges from CreateSpace provided that the required files are submitted as 'camera-ready' documents, one for the interior of the book, and one for the cover art.

CreateSpace does not check for spelling, grammar, or any other writing errors within the content. The two submitted files are only checked for compatibility with the printing or online distribution process for the size of book selected.

The author, you, assumes all responsibility for the accuracy of the files. What you submit is what gets distributed. The author's cost to publish can be zero because no professional help is sought and paid for along the way.

We assume here that the interior of the book has been completed using a text entry tool such as Microsoft Word and that only the book cover art is now preventing submittal for publication.

Help for those that still need to do final preparation and formatting of the interior file is a subject for another day and another book. The text file could be formatted, for example, similar to this book with chapter headers and footers and proper gutter spacing (the extra margin space on the side where pages are bound) for even and odd pages.

Cover art created with the process described in this book has been submitted and checked out on the CreateSpace platform. Files for Kindle are simple derivatives generated automatically by Amazon or easily adapted with some customization by the author.

This book will show how to design cover artwork using the simplest of tools: template information available from CreateSpace, a desktop PC, PowerPoint to compose the cover art, and Adobe's PDF (Portable Document Format) document reader with which to save the final document. The artwork is generated using text and color blocks plus pictures provided by the author.

CreateSpace accepts interior text files in several formats but cover art only as a PDF file. This book will show how to set up PowerPoint to export its contents as a high resolution PDF document. Other publishing platforms use a similar approach. Cover art composed as shown in subsequent chapters should also be compatible with platforms other than Amazon's CreateSpace.

Although this author prefers descriptive textual narrative written in complete sentences, much of the instruction material that follows is best conveyed concisely as a list of bulleted instruction lines. This book will use a mix of these two styles.

An example book cover will be generated by the end of this book. This can then be easily duplicated and adapted by readers to create artwork for a custom book cover.

Preface

The final demonstration of success is in fact the creation of cover art for this book. This was done using the simple tools described above.

The cover is generated and printed in color. The source illustrations imported into the interior of this book are mostly color images. However, the interior file will be printed in black and white. To keep printing costs down and to minimize the price of this book the original color elements were converted to grayscale images suitable for black and white printing.

Some of the images in the interior of the book are not quite up to the same quality standards that have been applied to the cover artwork.

Most of the procedural steps to create cover art involve instructions to be carried out on a computer. These are best conveyed by using actual computer screen shots. The quality of such images, their resolution as normally measured in pixels, is less than optimal. Predictably the subpar quality will cause some blurriness. Hopefully the images are still clear enough to fulfill their intended purpose.

I hope that you will judge this book literally by its cover. After all, that's what this book was all about.

Chapter 1 – Book Cover Art Overview

You've written what you hope will be a blockbuster novel. Or maybe it was a "How To" book, something that every handyperson needs to know. It could be that cookbook stuffed with recipes for food that gave you comfort since you were a child tugging at your mama's apron.

Somehow, you figured out how to capture all those words floating around your head and managed to type them into a computer. You even figured out how to insert pictures in your manuscript knowing that online book readers can be served text only, pictures only, or a combination of the two. You were also hoping that your hard copy publisher can print a text file with embedded grayscale pictures with apparently no extra effort or cost as compared to a file containing only text.

If you have checked out Amazon's CreateSpace as a publishing platform then you already know that what was described above is exactly what they offer to their clients. They also publish full color books but with higher printing costs and higher book prices. The choice, driven by the contents of the book, is yours.

With the interior text file complete, you are now anxious to get your book online and start watching that royalty stream come in.

You've used your text editor, Microsoft Word in most cases, to catch and correct spelling errors and simple grammatical errors. You know you can get your old high school English teacher to read over your manuscript to fix the trickier syntax errors and to critically review your work for clarity of thought as well as for self-consistency within the story.

You now feel confident that the interior text file is ready to be shipped to the publisher.

But you are now at a fork in the road. You need a cover for your book. You think that doing this job is a little beyond what you can do yourself.

You do a little research and find that there are many sources available to design a professional book cover for you – for a fee. These service providers also offer to review the interior text file and edit and repair any errors within it – also for quickly escalating fees.

But, wait, you got your English teacher or your nerdy sister in law to do a final check and correction of your manuscript. All you need to get ready for publishing is a cover design. But you don't want to spend money right now for professional help because that royalty revenue stream has not yet started.

This book is for you.

It will show you a step by step procedure with which to create a professional book cover.

To create cover art masterpieces that will showcase the nuggets of knowledge embedded within the pages you will need some computer graphics tools.

The goal of this book is to teach you to use the simplest of tools, one presumably available to anyone that has had to cope with capturing and presenting ideas for a regular day job before becoming an "author". That tool is Microsoft's PowerPoint that came with your Microsoft Office suite.

PowerPoint used as a platform to compose pictures and text as required for book cover artwork has some limitations. Those are pointed out in this book. More importantly, workarounds are identified and explained.

Sure, better tools like Adobe Photoshop may not require the workarounds that PowerPoint needs. But the goal was to not spend additional money at this time to buy additional software. You would also have to consider the additional time and effort to come up the learning curve enough to use Photoshop or similar software proficiently enough for this task.

CreateSpace provides several solutions to the problem of how to create a book cover without incurring any cost.

The simplest approach is to choose one of their cover art solutions from a collection of pre-defined formats. The collection contains templates with all the cover's essential elements. Their design platform offers opportunity for customization. This includes choices of themes and color schemes.

Using these pre-programmed templates is by far the least painful approach to creating your cover. You need no external tools since everything is done online. You will need a picture or two if you wish to embed them into these standard templates. The pictures can be used as background art or for inclusion of a snapshot of you, the author, on the back page.

One of the drawbacks with cover art that comes out of these pre-formatted cover templates is that the end product is fairly simple. Even though there are choices along the way, the end products have a similar and familiar appearance. They are easy to spot when your cover is displayed online, giving an early indication that your book got self-published by absolutely the lowest path of resistance and pain. There is nothing wrong with that, maybe for your first or your first couple of books.

An example of cover art generated using a CreateSpace template is shown below.

The standard template was embellished as best as possible by including a photograph as background for the front cover. The design of this cover art was constrained by the predefined appearance and location of elements such as the book title and the author name.

Still, considering that little time and effort was invested in creating it, the results do not appear too amateurish, a credit to CreateSpace for providing such tools online.

Cover art created using pre-formatted CreateSpace template

But at some point in time, you want more. You want that cover to scream "YOU", something that YOU totally generated. It may not look much different from the artwork shown above, but you want total control of where each element is placed and how it is formatted for best appearance.

You want to reflect your thoughts of how to best attract attention to your creation between the covers and you don't want it to look like dozens of other books that used the same preformatted template.

You want to create all the elements that show up on the cover pages. You want to combine them according to a design that you have in mind. You want to find a way to place each element correctly in relation to all the other elements and you want to find a way to upload to your publisher a "camera ready" document of the proper size for your book.

You want to create your own custom cover art solution from scratch. For me that point was reached by the time I got to my second book, after having used a pre-formatted template for the first one shown as an example above.

Before going further, let us look again at a typical book cover. It's similar in layout to the example already shown, but it was created from the ground up.

Such artwork is ultimately only one page that will be printed on a single sheet of cover stock paper. The size of this page has to be designed to precisely cover the front of the book, the back of the book, and the spine between front and back.

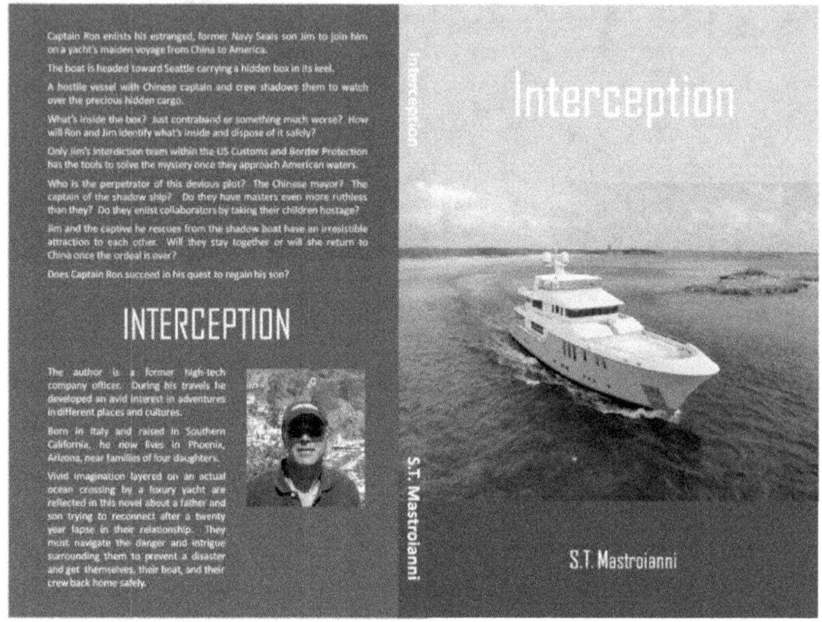

Custom book cover art

We need to identify the components contained within the artwork to help point the way to where we are going in the rest of this book.

You can easily identify the complete back page section. The elements contained within it are a text block at the top with a few teaser sentences about what's inside the book, the book title in the center of the page, and a few paragraphs about the author. An author photograph was also included. One additional element, a white rectangle block was included as a placeholder but was removed from the final cover art, leaving the space in the lower right hand corner of the back page. This space is reserved for the publisher to insert a UPC product code. CreateSpace will find this space, or even the white block if you leave it in anywhere on the page as long as it is of the specified size. CreateSpace will fill this area with your unique UPC code.

All the elements of the back page have been overlaid on a single, colored rectangle.

The boundaries of the front page are not so easy to spot. The reason is that in this example the front page design also includes the elements that will be wrapped around onto the spine of the book.

The spine artwork could be composed as its own picture or text blocks overlaid on its own background picture or color block.

An option for the spine design is to let the front page or the back page imagery wrap over it. The front page wrap was used in this example.

The title and author text blocks that CreateSpace requires to be placed on the spine (for books thicker than one hundred and one pages) are placed on the extended front cover artwork such that they correctly land on the center of the book spine. These text blocks have been rotated ninety degrees to create vertical text.

The front cover art contains a background picture plus text blocks for title and author name. The background picture is what really determines the visual appeal of your book. You can search the web and find publically shared (not copyright restricted) poster-like images that evoke what's in your book. Or, as in this example, you can use a high definition photo that you own or which you got from someone else after you obtain their "permission to use".

The size of the front and back covers are easy to determine. If, for example, you intend to publish a paperback using the most common size, six inches wide by nine inches tall, then each of those two areas of the cover artwork will have dimensions of six inches by nine inches, with a slight exception.

Here is the reason for the exception. When the book is manufactured, the pages including the covers must start out a little bigger than the end product. They are brought to their correct size during a final trim process. The trimming has some imprecision in it as paper or cutter may shift before the actual shearing of the cover and interior pages takes place. For this reason, the cover artwork is required to be somewhat larger than the end product. The excess space, which must be covered by the artwork, is called the "bleed" area.

The "bleed" area is applied to the total <u>width</u> of the cover art (the width of back cover, plus the spine, plus front cover), as well as to the <u>height</u> direction (top to bottom of covers and spine).

The width for the portion of cover art contributed by the front and back pages is determined immediately when the decision is made as to the size of the published book. For the example chosen, a six by nine inch book, this dimension is the sum of the widths of the two covers plus the extra amount required for the "bleed" area. The one additional dimension that must be added is the width of the spine. This dimension is variable.

The width of the spine is determined by the thickness of the combined pages that will be assembled between the covers.

To get the spine width we need to know the number of pages in the book and the thickness of each page. This number is therefore specific to each unique book and can only be calculated after the interior text file is finished, the paper stock selected, and the pages counted. Currently CreateSpace offers "white" and "cream" paper stock. Cream colored paper is slightly thicker than white paper.

Hold some of these thoughts in mind but don't let troublesome details confuse you. They will be clearly explained in subsequent chapters.

We can calculate all the required cover art dimensions long before we open up a blank PowerPoint worksheet using knowledge of the components that will be embedded within it. These have already been pointed out: width and height of the book, number of pages in the book, and thickness of one sheet of paper multiplied by the number of pages.

CreateSpace can optionally provide you a dimensional template containing placeholders for all these dimensions. The template can be generated after the interior text file has been completed and the paper type has been selected. You can navigate within the CreateSpace website to find this feature, or you can use the web address listed later in this book.

This starting template can be used as an under-layer that will guide us during the job of creating the actual cover art composed of text blocks, color blocks, and pictures. Note that this template only has dimensions within it. It is not the same sort of templates as the CreateSpace cover art template illustrated earlier. The previous one had dimensions of your eventual book plus starting point artwork components such as picture placeholders and various text blocks for title, author, etc.

The dimensional CreateSpace template for the custom book cover art illustrated earlier is shown below.

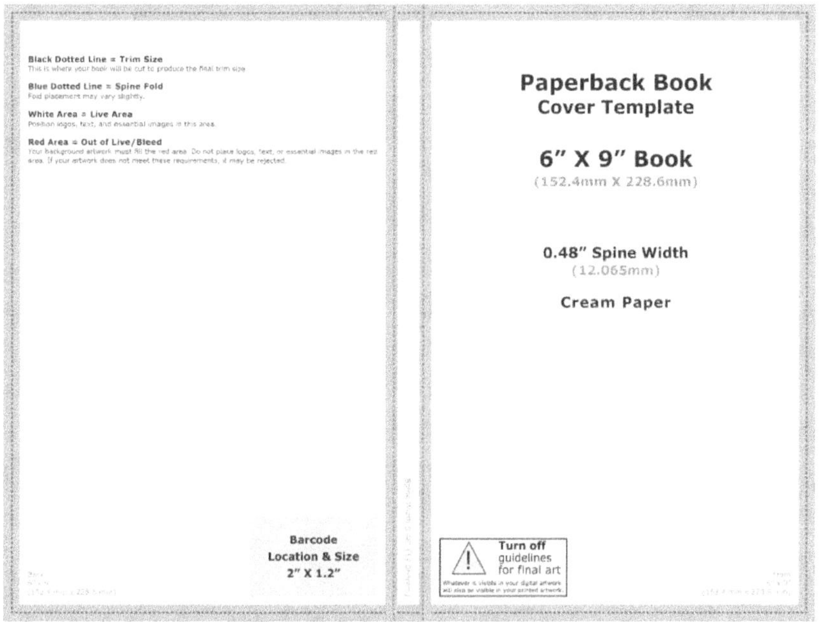

Cover art dimensional template generated by CreateSpace

Note that the template conveys all the necessary information needed to begin to generate the composed artwork.

The spine width in this example, 0.48 inches, was calculated by CreateSpace for a book containing one hundred ninety pages of cream colored paper.

CreateSpace makes this template available to the user in two formats, a PDF file and a PNG (picture format) file. Visually they are identical. The version pasted in this book for this example is the PNG file. This is easily imported into PowerPoint as an image, as it was easily imported into the Word document that you are now reading. Importing the PDF version of this image is not so straightforward with the free version of Adobe's PDF viewer that exists on most computers.

The task to compose your artwork then is nothing more than importing or generating a template like the image shown above, one specifically tailored to your book after you have finished the interior text file and decided on a book size, into a PowerPoint worksheet which can then be used to aggregate all the visual components.

Once we have generated the cover art we are ready to submit that single page document to CreateSpace. Their software environment accepts only files in PDF format, so as the very last step we will need to save the PowerPoint file as a PDF document.

Provided that the page meets the dimensional requirements for compatibility with the interior part of the book then CreateSpace will open the gate to allow actual printing of the book. Their analysis is only applied to dimensional properties and to compatibility of the other component elements. The visual aspects, what your cover art shows, has been determined solely by what you chose to place in it as text blocks, color blocks, and picture elements. How to properly do these tasks, within the capabilities of PowerPoint, will be explained in the subsequent chapters of this book.

Chapter 2 – Cover Art Templates

Task instructions will be conveyed as a "bulleted" to-do list. In the material that follows, *italics* are used for words that appear in the referenced computer menus or popup screens. They should appear on your computer as shown by the *italics* text in these instructions. Minor differences may show up for different versions of software.

We have already seen a dimensional template generated using CreateSpace. The resulting image was included at the end of the last chapter.

The steps needed to generate that template are shown below.

Cover Art Template Generated By CreateSpace

- Open a browser (Microsoft's *Internet Explorer* or *Edge*, Google *Chrome*, etc.) to the following CreateSpace web address:
  - *https://www.createspace.com/Help/Book/Artwork.do*
- Fill out the form:

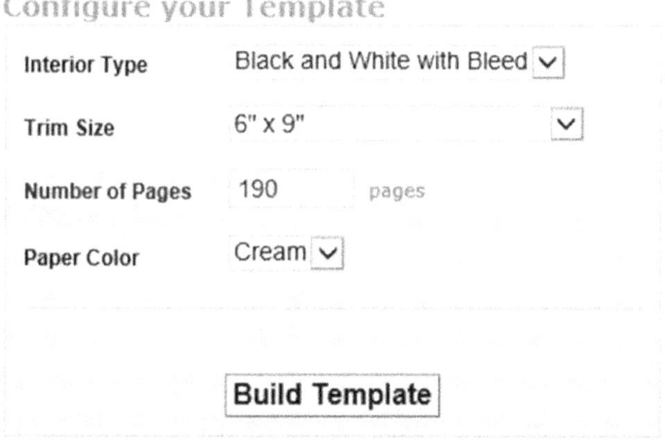

- Click on *Build Template.*
  - CreateSpace will return a *Zip* folder containing a *PNG Template* and a *PDF Template* document
- Click to *Download* Zip file. When the menu pops up, choose *Save as,* and identify where to save it on your computer, somewhere that you will remember for later retrieval. Using the folder with all your other book material would be good.
- Navigate to the downloaded Zip Folder:
  - the name of the folder is *BookCover6x9_Cream_190*
- Open the folder and then open either the *PNG Template* or the *PDF Template* to see what CreateSpace has created for you. You will see the image below:

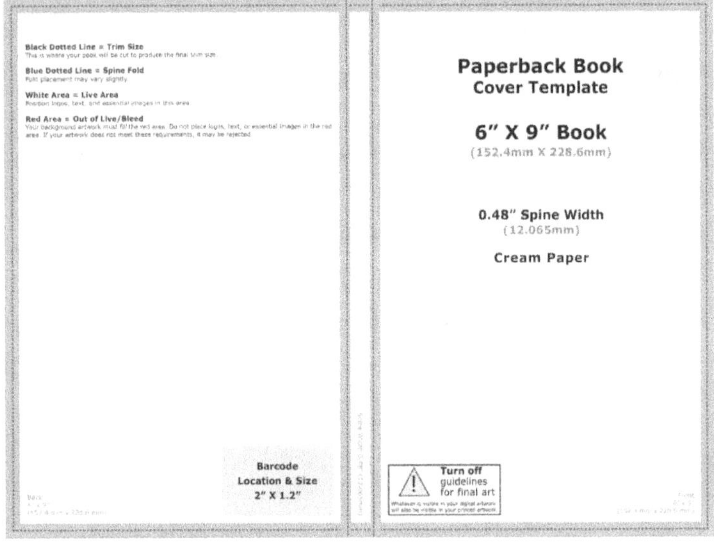

- Note the rectangle in the lower right hand corner of the back cover. This is a 2" x 1.2" placeholder for where CreateSpace will place the UPC product barcode. The location shown is the preferred one, but it can be anywhere on the back cover. CreateSpace will find it and fill it in. This element can either be a white rectangle located anywhere or simply a reserved space free of any other text located as shown on the template.

We could use the dimensional template automatically generated using CreateSpace as a starting point for our cover art.

We choose instead to generate our own because it will make it much easier to generate the overlaying artwork.

The automatically generated template is one single image. The version that we will generate has individual placeholders for each element. We will set up PowerPoint to allow elements to 'snap' into position relative to the placeholders. In this way we will produce finished artwork with elements precisely aligned to each other, with no visible gaps. This will be evident later in the book.

Cover Art Template Information Generated By Author

- Select dimensions of book to be published:
  - 6" x 9" is the most popular size and will be used here
- "Bleed" area (extra cover space to allow for book trimming):
  - 0.125" on each edge of composite cover art
- **Height** of composite cover art is:
  - (height of the book) + (bottom "bleed") + (top "bleed")
  - 9" + 0.125" + 0.125" = 9.25"
- Thickness of one page printed by CreateSpace:
  - white paper: 0.002252" per page
  - cream paper: 0.0025" per page
  - example design will use cream paper
- Number of pages in book used for this example:
  - 190
- Thickness of book (width of spine):
  - (number of pages) x (thickness of one page):
  - 190 x 0.0025 = 0.48"
- **Width** of composed cover art:
  - (width of back cover) + (width of spine) + width of front cover) + (left edge "bleed") + (right edge "bleed")

- o   6" + 0.48" + 0.6" + 0.125" + 0.125" = 12.73"
- Template with dimensions as shown was generated with PowerPoint. How it is done will be covered in Chapter 4.
- Later chapters will also address the following <u>extremely important</u> two points:
  - o   how to do the proper PowerPoint *Page Setup* <u>prior</u> to starting any work in order to preserve image resolution of objects placed on the worksheet
  - o   how to properly *Save* the PowerPoint worksheet to preserve maximum image resolution

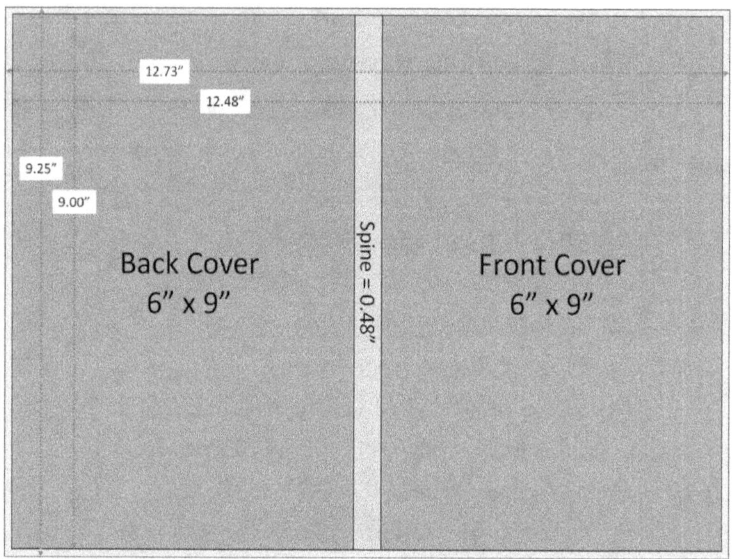

Custom generated template image

- Note the 0.125' "bleed" area on each edge. This area must be covered by artwork.
- The appearance is very different compared to the CreateSpace template, but the information contained in it is identical. Either form could be used as a starting point on a PowerPoint worksheet that will ultimately create the finished cover art, but the custom approach has advantages.

Chapter 3 – Working With PowerPoint

PowerPoint as installed by Microsoft Office has several limitations when used to create high resolution cover art. The motivation to find ways to still use it for this apparently misfit purpose is that it is available to most people with access to a computer.

The inherent shortcomings are more severe with older versions. Gradual improvements have been made as PowerPoint progressed from versions 2003 through several iterations to version 2016.

These limitations show up while we work with the PowerPoint worksheet and when we try to export the finished document in a format as required by publishers such as CreateSpace.

The main purpose for this book is to show workarounds to prevent or minimize the identified limitations so that we can still produce adequate cover art.

This chapter pursues three goals:

- To define the minimum image quality useful for printing. Each step of the art creation process should then meet or exceed this minimum standard. This includes collecting individual visual elements, composing the artwork, saving the file, and exporting the final document as a PDF page.
- To convey a basic understanding of image resolution requirements of:
  - each element within the cover art, and
  - the resolution requirement of the artwork document as a whole

- To show how to set up the page format on a PowerPoint worksheet <u>before</u> any elements, pictures, or text blocks are placed on it. Changing the setup after objects have been placed will distort their appearance (aspect ratio) as well as disturb their placement.

Although the focus of this book is on identifying PowerPoint shortcomings and defining workarounds, we will along the way also point out "best practices" to facilitate grouping of visual elements and improve their combined visual appearance.

Image Resolution Requirement for Printing - Common Practice

Print shops generally have guidelines for quality of images so that they can render good printed results.

Such quality has traditionally been specified in terms of dpi, dots per inch. As applied to modern digital photographs, a more appropriate term is ppi, pixels per inch when an image's intrinsic pixel count is spread over the space over which it is to be printed.

For our purposes the two terms can be used interchangeably since we understand that we are only considering images that will be printed as hard copy.

Most print shops prefer 300dpi (or 300ppi) resolution in order to achieve unquestionable photographic image quality in a print.

Evaluating the suitability of an image is then nothing more than taking its pixel count in either its width or its height dimension and dividing it by the number of inches that the respective width or height will cover when printed.

In reality it is generally accepted that resolution of 200dpi will also achieve photographic quality in print, provided that you start out with a good quality photo (for example, no image degradation because the photo was taken with a subpar camera lens).

Therefore, even though the print shop guidelines may ask for 300dpi, photos will print just fine with resolution down to 200dpi.

It is a goal of this book to show a process by which images that start out with resolution of at least 200dpi can be imported into a cover art design, preserved at this or greater quality throughout the steps required to generate the composite artwork, and to be able to export them to a publisher at this or greater quality.

Achieving 300dpi is a worthy goal and attempts will be made to do this at each step of the way. Achieving 200dpi will still be considered a success in view of the simple tools used.

Image Resolution Requirement for CreateSpace Book Covers

- For optimum image clarity CreateSpace <u>prefers</u> that all graphics submitted have a resolution of at least 300dpi. Artwork with lower resolution will still be accepted and printed.

- We will strive for 300dpi resolution and compromise only when restricted by the tools we use.

- Submitted artwork with elements containing less than 200dpi resolution will be flagged. CreateSpace does not identify offending images. You have to figure out which ones caused the flag to be thrown.

- The fact that CreateSpace considers resolution above 200dpi as acceptable seems to be consistent with common printing practices described in the prior section.

- The entire cover art document must be generated and preserved at the desired resolution during the entire creation process. We have to consider each image element individually, as well s the composed artwork in its entirety.

- Artwork resolution should at the very least be at 200dpi, above the point where CreateSpace throws a warning flag. This is the subject of several subsequent chapters.

- Setting up the PowerPoint worksheet, compatible with the desired image resolution is covered in this chapter.

- CreateSpace does not accept cover art as a PowerPoint document or even such documents saved as PNG or JPEG images. They only accept a single PDF (Portable Document Format) page containing the composite cover art.
- PowerPoint can export its file content to a PDF format, but it has an inherent limitation which must be overcome prior to conversion in order to preserve at least the minimum level of resolution. Fulfilling this requirement will be addressed in Chapter 9.

Cover Image Example – Introduction of Resolution Aspects

- If we want to cover the entire front or back cover of a 6"x 9" book with a background picture then we should import an image with at least:
    - (6" x 300) x (9" x 300) = (1,800 x 2,700) pixels
- Images of this quality may be generated with a recent digital camera or may be obtained from the internet for free or for a fee. Check out the resolution before you use them!
- A PowerPoint worksheet can hold such high resolution pictures, either as PNG or JPEG images, while you work with it but it has limitations as to how many pixels it can save or export to another application such as a PDF reader.
- PowerPoint (at least some versions of it) may conspire against you each step of the way, for example, compressing images (and shrinking resolution) when you save the file. Care must be taken during the creation and saving process to avoid such compression. How to minimize such negative effects during the *Save* step will be addressed in Chapter 4.

***

Setting PowerPoint Worksheet - Page Setup Attributes

The PowerPoint worksheet must be sized properly. It must optimize the number of pixels that can be captured and preserved. We will explain below how it could be too small or too big.

- Artwork should be designed at a scale of at least 1:1 (actual size) otherwise it would have to be scaled up to fill the book cover, in this way reducing the printed resolution relative to the images placed on the worksheet.

- CreateSpace states in their General Guidelines that artwork should be submitted on 18" x 12" or 19" x 13" pages.

- CreateSpace downscales the printable area to match it to the actual size of the cover. This assumes that we submit a document with resolution of 300dpi or greater. The artwork will then meet or exceed the minimum criteria when downscaled (there will be more pixels than necessary when the printing area is reduced relative to the original layout). But creating such a large page (18" x 12" or greater) while trying to preserve resolution is an issue with PowerPoint.

- A PowerPoint <u>key</u> <u>limitation</u> will show up when we export the final document as a PDF file for printing. PowerPoint has an absolute upper limit for the total number of dots (or pixels) that each slide can export:
  - 3,072 dots in the largest dimension of the document
  - for landscape orientation, that would be the width

- To preserve the highest resolution possible in landscape orientation the worksheet should ideally then have a width of:
  - about 10" and not greater
  - (3,072 dots)/ 10" = 307 dpi (defaulted to 300dpi by PowerPoint)

- But a width of 10" is too small to house our cover art at 1:1 scale.

- We could use CreateSpace's recommended size of 18" x 12".

- But the 18" width cannot be supported at 300dpi:

- o (3,072 dots)/ 18" = 171 dpi
  - o this falls short of our stated goal of 200dpi minimum
- The size we will choose is just enough to hold the composite artwork laid out exactly to the size required by the book cover, 1:1, with a little extra border around each edge:
  - o from the earlier template, artwork = 12.73" x 9.25"
  - o choose a PowerPoint sheet size of 14" x 10"
- If we were to fill the worksheet edge to edge, then we have already reduced the available resolution to less than 300dpi
  - o (3072 dots) / 14" = 219dpi
  - o this falls within our stated goal of 200dpi minimum
  - o since we will not fill the worksheet edge to edge then we have wasted some of our precious resolution on empty space (the extra space around the edges), but we have tried to keep this to a reasonable amount
- If we incur no further degradation, then 219dpi will be our submitted resolution. This is less than the preferred 300dpi but greater that the 200dpi that we defined as success considering the simple tools used.
- We are so far achieving our goal, but we have to check it against one more PowerPoint limitation.
- Another PowerPoint <u>key</u> <u>limitation</u> is also encountered when exporting the final document as PDF for publishing. It has an absolute upper limit for resolution, applied to the entire exported image and therefore to any element within it.
  - o 96dpi is the default preset within PowerPoint; unless this is improved, this would be a catastrophic 'show-stopper'
  - o the entire Chapter 9 is devoted to installing a fix for this problem; PowerPoint's export resolution will be bumped up to 300dpi
  - o with the fix applied, the resulting 300dpi export resolution will exceed the 219ppi resolution limit that we have already built into our cover art worksheet

- This author has submitted to CreateSpace worksheets smaller than their stated preference for 18" x 12". This has caused no flags or other reported issues.

***

Now that we understand the underlying reasons for our choice for document size, we are ready to set up the page format:

- Open PowerPoint to start a blank worksheet.
- Navigate upper commands ribbon to *Design*.
- Select *Page Setup*.
- The following popup menu will show up:

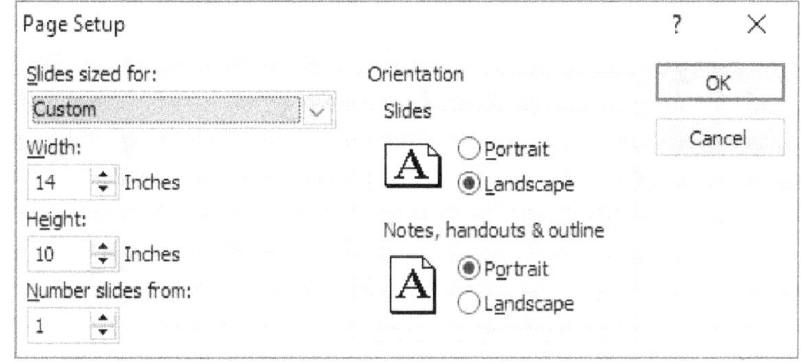

- Select *Custom* size, and enter *14* for *Width* and *10* for *Height*

***

Setting PowerPoint Worksheet 'Snap Objects' Feature

An important aspect of how PowerPoint objects land on the worksheet is the concept of an imaginary grid underneath the live objects. New elements snap to this invisible grid when placed on the worksheet. They each align to the grid so in theory they can each align to each other.

The above reflects the most common use of PowerPoint. The method works for large objects that do not require exact positioning relative to each other. Misalignment of the objects occurs if their height and width dimensions do not end up being exact multiples of the grid spacing. This is not ideal for our work because occasionally it will result in visible gaps between objects when we intended such objects to butt up exactly to their neighbor. This mode must be changed.

- PowerPoint in its startup mode defaults to a *Snap Objects to Grid* mode, with the grid normally preset at 0.83".

- For cover art, a better mode is to select *Snap Objects to Other Objects*, so that each element of the cover art can precisely snap/align to other elements, without regard to any underlying grid.

- To select the *Snap to Other Objects* mode, place cursor anywhere on the blank PowerPoint sheet we just created and right click. A popup menu will appear which contains the item *Grid and Guides*. Select this item and it will show as below.

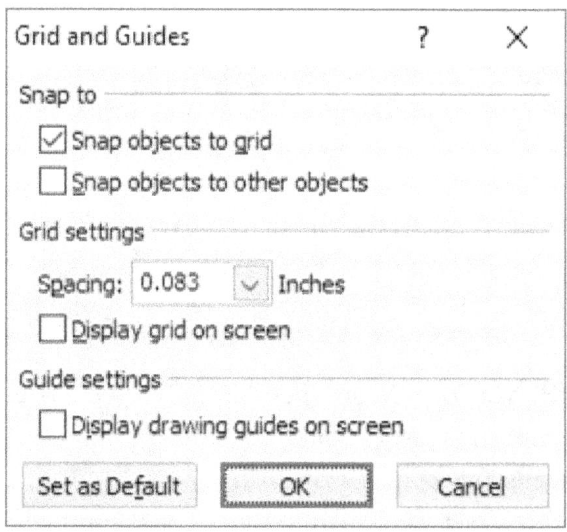

- Unselect the *Snap objects to grid* and select the *Snap objects to other objects*.

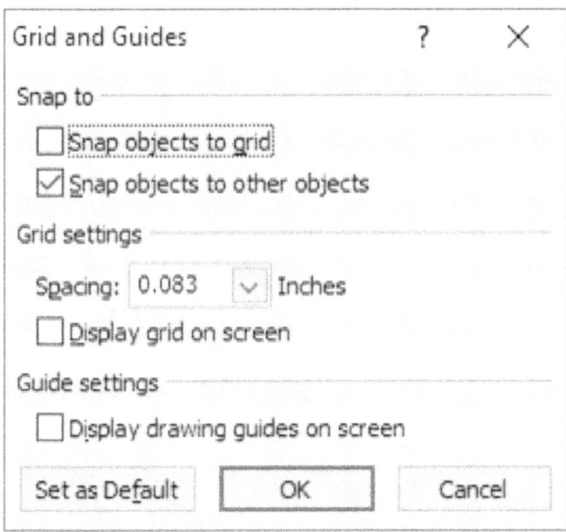

- Click *OK*.
- We now have a PowerPoint worksheet properly set up to contain the cover artwork and preserve as much resolution as possible.
- Once these attributes have been set (including the snap feature just defined) they will stay with the document on which they were defined throughout the life of the document (the many *Saves* that will follow).
- However, when a new PowerPoint document is opened, the settings for that new document will default to the presets. They must then be modified as desired by the user.

We are done with setting up the PowerPoint worksheet and with selecting how objects will be positioned relative to each other.

Chapter 4 – Import/Generate Template Info

Before we go further, we need to address 'color' vs. 'black and white' for objects that we will include in the cover art.

The CreateSpace cover will be printed in color. Therefore the imagery on the printed cover should look as colorful as the images that you see on your PowerPoint worksheet.

This is in contrast to the file that normally defines the interior of a book.

CreateSpace currently charges no fee when submitting your interior file whether or not it contains color elements. Colors will be retained for books published in color otherwise they will be defaulted to 'black and white'.

The interior of this book was obviously published in 'black and white'. This was done to minimize cost.

The term 'black and white' needs an explanation. Although the publisher only uses black ink, it can produce embedded images with grayscale hues by using a dot screening (software) process.

Printing a book with color pages is much more expensive than black and white. This is reflected in Amazon's cost to publish, making it necessary for the author to specify a much higher price, above Amazon's break even cost, before any royalties can be earned.

This book's interior text file contains pictures and computer screen shots. Many of the source images were in color. These images were converted to grayscale before placing them within the text file. This was somewhat tedious. They could have been left as color in the manuscript. CreateSpace automatically converts them to grayscale before print time, but this author wanted to see what the resulting images look like prior to submitting the file.

***

We are now ready to start work on a PowerPoint worksheet to create the cover art.

The first step is to generate a template. We will use the custom template information that we generated earlier in this example.

- If not already open, open a PowerPoint blank worksheet with page dimensions defined in the *Page Setup* menu and select *Snap Objects to Other Objects* as previously detailed.

- If the ruler does not show at the top of the worksheet, navigate the upper command ribbon to *View*, click to select, and then check the box next to *Ruler* within the *Show/Hide* command block.

- Navigate back to the PowerPoint *Home* menu, where all the drawing commands now show up. We assume familiarity with placing items such as lines, rectangles, and text block objects from this menu onto the worksheet.

- Select the *line* icon from the *Drawing* menu and place a vertical line on the worksheet to cover as much of the page as possible, top to bottom, without going outside the page. Align this line with the *0* on the ruler at the top. This will give us a center line marker. Hold the *Shift* key down while drawing the line. This will keep it perfectly vertical.

- Next draw a rectangle on the blank portion of the worksheet. Any size will do for now.

- Keeping the rectangle selected (highlighted for editing), click on the *Shape Fill* menu item in the tool ribbon. From the pop menu, select a color. This will become the placeholder for the book spine.

- With the rectangle still selected, click on the *Shape Outline*. From the popup menu, select *No Outline*.

- Right click on the rectangle. From the popup menu, select *Format Shape*.

- Slide the *Transparency* control to around 30% then click *CLOSE*.

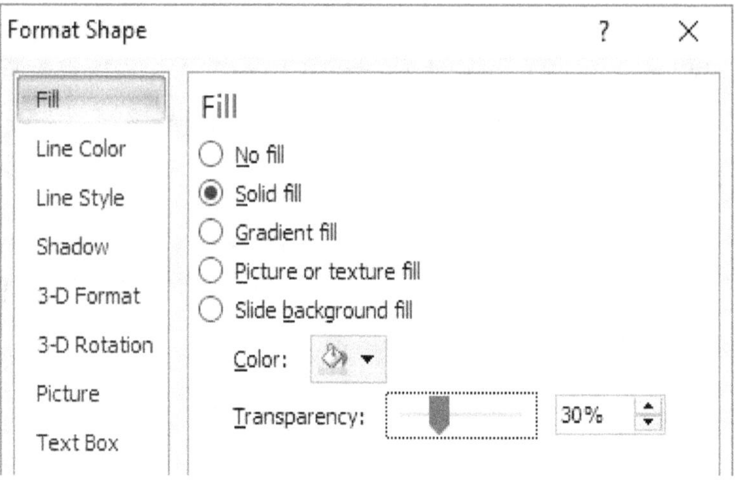

- Why the transparency setting on this block and subsequent ones? It is good practice to do this so that any other object that may accidentally end up layered underneath it can still be visible even if totally overlaid by this object.

- A good reminder at this point: if objects mistakenly get placed on top of each other in a sequence that is not what we had in mind, they can be manipulated above or below other objects by selecting the object we wish to move and then using the *Order Object* within the *Arrange* menu. This menu shows up in the tool ribbon at the top of PowerPoint's *Home* menu.

- Right click on the rectangle again. From the popup menu select *Size and Position*. Type in the dimensions from our earlier template work, 9.25" for *height* to cover the 9" book cover plus "bleed" and the exact 0.48" for the spine *width*.

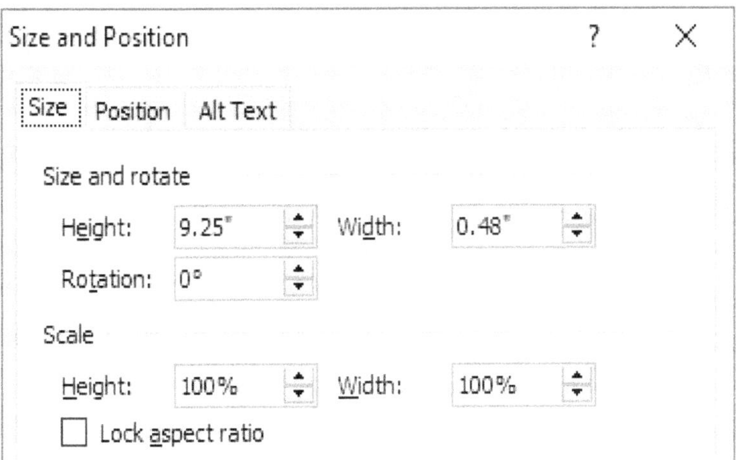

- Close the *Size and Position* window. Now select the rectangle by left clicking and holding the mouse button, and slide the rectangle near the center line marker we put on the sheet. The rectangle will snap to the center line if you just get it close enough. Slide up and down to "eyeball" center top to bottom on worksheet, trying to leave an equal amount of space beyond the spine rectangle space at top and bottom of worksheet.

- We could have placed a horizontal line precisely located in the center, top to bottom, of the worksheet. This would allow us to place our template objects centered top to bottom as we have done left to right. This has been found to be unnecessary, as any inaccuracy created by "eyeballing" seems to be handled by CreateSpace's software.

- At this point, you should have a worksheet with the center spine template object, and a center line. (Only a small portion of the top of the image is shown below).

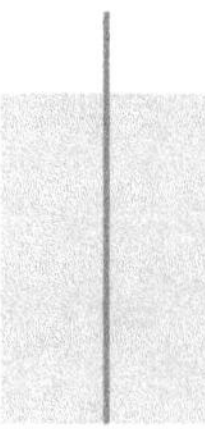

- Follow the same procedures to create a front cover artwork template. Select any color you like (this object will not be retained in the final artwork), set the *Shape Outline* to *No Outline*, and set *Transparency* also to about 30%. Use the sizing command to specify the required dimensions of 6.125" for *width* and 9.25" for *height*. Copy and paste the object to generate a duplicate for the back cover. Snap the two new objects to the right and left of the spine rectangle. Objects should snap, perfectly aligned to each other.

The template shown so far was created by using only basic information about the size of the book. This image will be used in subsequent chapters as we generate or import all the visual elements that will comprise the finished book cover artwork.

Alternatively, as we have already mentioned before, we could use the template generated for us by CreateSpace.

Using the CreateSpace template might appear easier than creating our own from the ground up. It consists of nothing more than importing the template image as a whole into a page (slide) of PowerPoint. But the approach demonstrated allowed us a better opportunity to understand how to configure PowerPoint and how to better understand the different elements of the composite book cover. Additionally, the placeholders for individual components will facilitate snapping in of actual art objects in order to align them perfectly.

We are ready to move on, to place actual cover visual elements on the dimensional template that we just generated. The custom template meticulously defined the elements and centered them (left to right, as CreateSpace requires) on a correctly sized PowerPoint worksheet.

Before we proceed, we should save the work we have created so far. Moving to that step runs into another limitation preconfigured into PowerPoint and which we must modify.

Putting a file away with a simple *Save* command invoke a hidden step that <u>may</u> compress images to keep files manageable by shrinking their size, and <u>will</u> compress images to fit within a maximum resolution that PowerPoint is able to save.

Compressing the images we have created so far would not be too harmful at this point because they are simple colored rectangles. It may, however, be a serious impediment in our quest to preserve resolution if the worksheet contained high resolution pictures.

We must insure that minimal compression takes place. There is not much we can do for PowerPoint's inherent resolution limit for saved files other than to make sure the setting is at the maximum resolution allowed. We can, however, uncheck the compression feature,

The followings steps describe what we can do.

Preserving Image Resolution When Saving PowerPoint Files

The workaround described below involves navigation within PowerPoint to the *Save as* command so that we can turn off the image compression feature if it is so defaulted and to make sure that the maximum *Save* resolution is selected.

We need to get in the habit of following this procedure before we begin to import pictures. Failure to prevent compression when saving a worksheet will result in loss of image quality. This cannot be recovered and the fix is to start over and re-import all your images.

The saving grace is that you only have to change the settings once when you first open the worksheet or before you start importing high resolution images. The settings will remain with the document from that point on.

Perform the following steps:

- Click on the *Office* button way at the upper left hand corner of your PowerPoint Document.
- Click on *Save As*.
- The following popup menu appears:

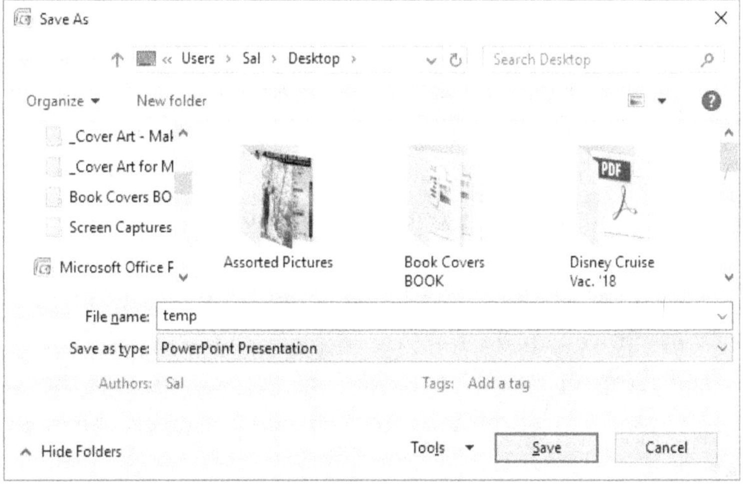

- Click on *Tools* at the bottom of the window. You will see a new popup menu. Click on *Compress Pictures...* and the following will show up:

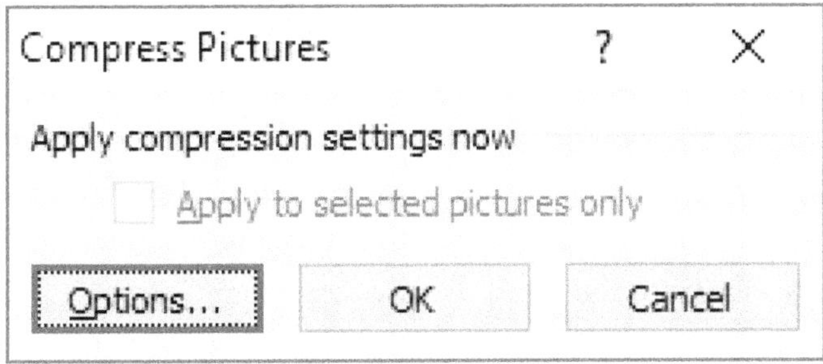

- Click on *Options* to see the following:

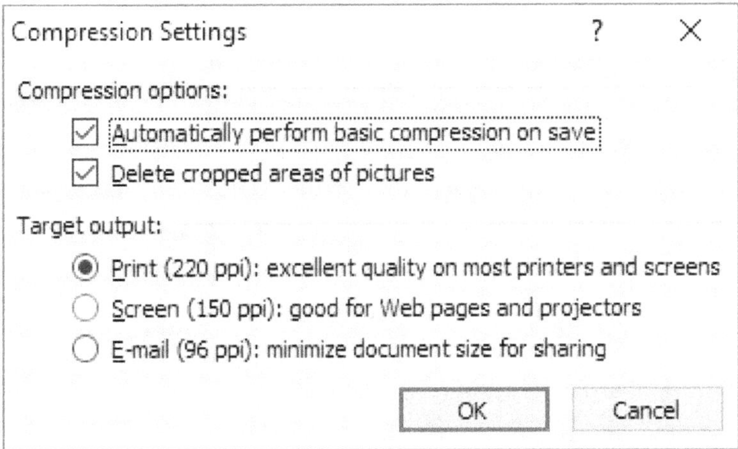

- Notice that the PowerPoint default setting when saving its documents is *Automatically perform basic compression on save*, with the output preset to the maximum that it will allow (220 ppi where ppi is pixels per inch, same as dots per inch).
- Uncheck the box for *Automatically perform basic compression on save*.
- Click *OK* and then *OK* again to put away the popup menus.
- Click on *Save*. The worksheet has been saved without compression and the maximum resolution allowed by PowerPoint.

- This setting will remain <u>on</u> <u>this</u> <u>document</u> during the entire life of this document.

- Whenever a new worksheet is opened, its *Save* settings will be in the default compress mode. You have to repeat the procedure above for the new document if you wish to preserve all resolution.

Notice that regardless of the compression setting PowerPoint will always generate an output with a maximum of 220dpi. The consequence is that from that first *Save* onward, resolution can never be greater than 220ppi.

Apparently the Microsoft PowerPoint software people consider this 220ppi value to be adequate for printing, consistent with prevailing practices at commercial print shops as stated earlier.

We might be tempted then to not worry about generating or importing any image objects with any greater resolution.

One reason to resist this temptation is to force ourselves to collect artwork images at a higher resolution for such times when either PowerPoint will improve and not have so many limitations, or when we might have evolved to use better software tools with which to compose cover art. For such cases we will then be able to update our final product simply by retrieving the original high resolution pictures, and re-composing the artwork.

Do not, however, lose track of the point of this book. The goals stated upfront were to use common tools at hand to create cover art at resolution considered acceptable by most printing houses. Visual quality, even under the restrictions imposed on us by the tools, can be verified as an example by the cover of this book.

NOTE: Concerning Different Versions of PowerPoint

The procedure for unsetting the compression feature shown above was performed using PowerPoint 2007. The compression setting was modified using the *Save As* command.

Newer versions of PowerPoint allow this feature to be set under the PowerPoint *Options* menu. In that case, the following may be used:

- Click on the *Office* button way at the upper left hand corner of your PowerPoint Document.
- Click on *PowerPoint Options*.
- The following popup menu appears:
    - only a portion of the menu is shown, for better legibility
    - note that the *Advanced* tab was selected
    - focus on the *Image Size and Quality* section: the *Do not compress image file* box should be checked and the *Set default target output* should be selected to the maximum value of *220ppi*

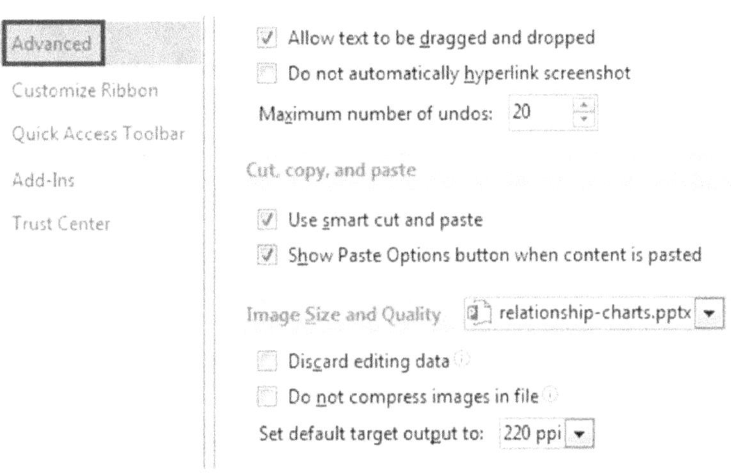

Chapter 5 – Importing Front Cover Picture

The image displayed on the front cover is probably the most important element of the cover art. This image should be of the highest resolution possible. Be careful if obtaining free pictures from image searches on the web. Owners of meaningful images are usually careful to preserve the high resolution version of their work and offer it for sale. If you download a picture that you wish to use, make sure that you check its resolution, the number of pixels it contains, before you commit to it.

Requirements for this critical element are explained below.

Importing A Picture For Front Cover Background
- The background picture for the front cover can be sized to cover the front cover only.
- In that case, the spine can be a color block which will ultimately contain the required book title and author name (required for books with thickness of 101 pages or greater).
- Alternatively, the front cover image can be designed to fill the cover plus the spine, if you wish the image to wrap around the spine of the book.
- In the example artwork developed in this book, the image will be sized to cover part of the front cover and the spine.
- We will need an image with a <u>width</u> of:
    - width of cover including "bleed" + width of spine = 6.125"+0.48" = 6.605"

- For 300dpi, a picture with the following minimum resolution in its <u>width</u> dimension:
    - 6.605" x 300dpi = 1982 pixels
- If we wanted to cover the entire height of the cover, then we would need a minimum resolution in its <u>height</u> dimension:
    - 9.25" x 300dpi = 2775 pixels
- The number of pixels shown is the desired minimum to meet our lofty goal of 300dpi.
- Additional pixels will not hurt. The limitations in our current process will simply discard them as excess pixels. But retention of high resolution images may be useful with future versions of software, should one wish to regenerate the artwork and resubmit it.
- If the image selected does not have the minimum number of pixels, then:
    - reduce the amount of space that it fills on the cover until the pixel count is adequate, or
    - use it anyway, but try to at least meet a 200dpi goal
    - recall that, due to limitations we have already encountered and more yet to come, the actual resolution preserved in the creation process may shrink down to a value less than 300dpi
- Recall also that CreateSpace will flag the artwork if the resolution falls below 200dpi, indicating that reduced resolution may cause image blur.
- For this example I have chosen an original photograph that has resolution of 4,007 x 2,913 pixels, more than enough to do the job. It is a landscape formatted picture. I do not intend to cover the entire page but to cover only the center section. The remainder of the space on the front cover will be filled by the title text block and the author text block.
- Select the picture and use the *Copy* and *Paste* commands to copy the image onto the PowerPoint worksheet.

- The image will appear to entirely cover the worksheet and then some… we need to shrink to the desired size.

- One method to do this is as follows: shrink it to fit within the workspace by dragging one of the corner handles, and then dragging the entire picture to snap to the left edge of the spine. We now have the image shown below. It's important to size the picture using only handles at the corner. If handles on the sides or top/bottom are used to resize, then the picture aspect ratio will be lost and the picture will look distorted compared to the original. Note that we have not accurately sized the picture yet… we have only roughly sized it and aligned its left edge where we want it.

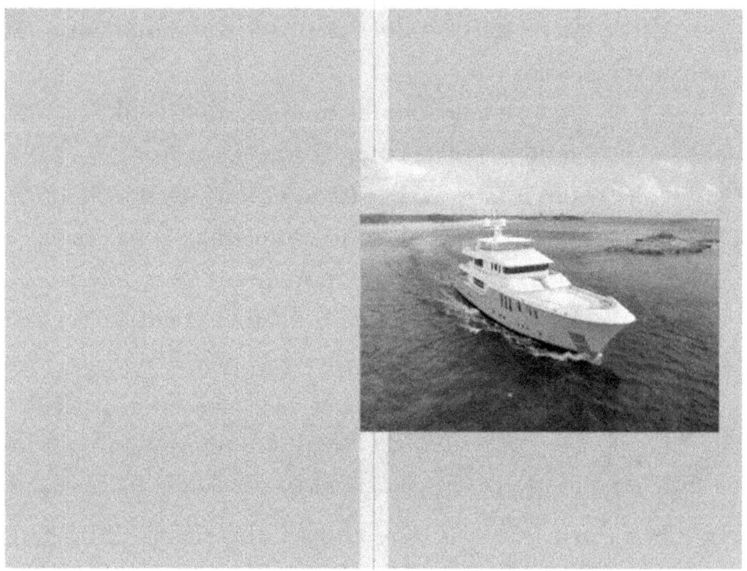

- Right click on the picture and choose *Size and Position* from the popup menu.

- The popup menu shown below will appear.

- Make sure that the check mark is in the *Lock aspect ratio* box and that a check mark is also in the *Relative to original picture size*. This will insure that the picture will shrink equally in width and height as it is being sized, so as to prevent a distorted picture.

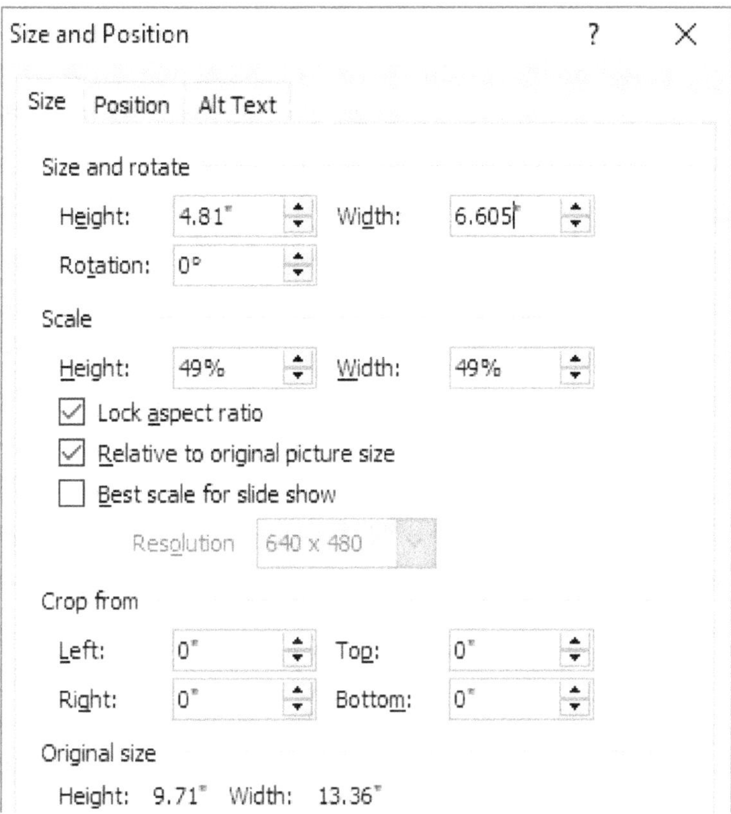

- You can see that in the case of the example picture used, the above action had the effect of shrinking it to 49% of its original size.

- No cropping was done on this picture, as it was decided to use it as is and tailor to it the other elements of the front cover.

- If cropping is necessary, to adjust the picture aspect ratio (height to width ratio) to fit a particular space, then refer to the Appendix in this book. This task, accomplished by scaling the number of pixels in either width or height, is carefully explained there.

- An alternative method to size the picture, since we know the exact dimension as built into the template, is to do the following:
  - o select the large picture that we imported into PowerPoint by left clicking on it if it isn't already selected; right click and the sizing menu shown above will pop up
  - o fill in the value for width to match the same value that we entered when we made the placeholder for the front cover (6.605")
  - o the image will be sized just right and it is now just a matter of snapping it to the left edge of the placeholder
  - o either method will give you the resulting picture shown below:

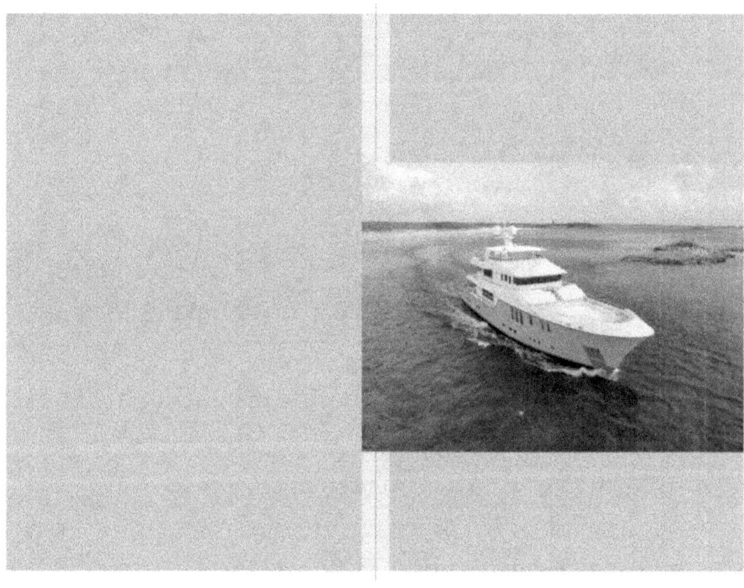

Picture is the only cover element so far. Notice it also covers part of the spine. All other images are template placeholders.

Chapter 6 – Front Cover Text Blocks

In this example we will only generate a title block and an author block. These are usually colored rectangles that contain the associated text. These rectangles can be of solid color if there is no need for them to allow viewing of an underlying image, or they can be defined with transparency so that the image below can bleed through the text blocks.

Modifying the transparency of a rectangle has already been covered in Chapter 4 and will not be repeated here.

Front Cover Title and Author Blocks

- We will now add a colored rectangle to house the book title.
- Draw any size rectangle on a blank spot of the worksheet (use the back cover area).
- As before, choose a color that you like (compatible with color scheme of front cover), and choose *No Outline*. Right click on rectangle and size it correctly:
    - the <u>width</u> is that of the page width + the "bleed" area at the right, 6.125" (which the computer rounds off to 6.13")
    - the <u>height</u> can be any arbitrary dimension for now
- Drag the rectangle to align its upper left corner to the upper right corner of the spine. Grab the handle on the bottom side of the rectangle and drag to snap it to the top side of the photograph. We now have the following image.

- Perform similar actions to generate and place a color rectangle to fill the remaining bottom space of the front cover artwork, this time snapping to the lower right corner of the spine.

- The following image will result:

- Note that the rectangles below and above the picture are now text blocks, overlaid over the page template rectangle.

- Notice also that the text blocks are centered on the front cover template. When we place the text centered within those blocks, they will be centered relative to the front cover.

- Duplicate (*copy* and *save*) on the worksheet the upper blank text block, leave the height as is, but size the width to the width of the spine. This will fill the upper part of the spine and appear as a continuation wraparound of the front cover.
  - spine width = 0.48"

- Do the same for the lower text block. This will cover the lower portion of the spine.

- Next we will place the book title and the author name within the colored blocks reserved for them. From the tool ribbon at the top of PowerPoint select the text tool (the icon that looks like a box with the letter *A* in it, contained within the *Drawing* submenu).

- Place the cursor within the Title block. Type in the text. Choose the *font* and *font size*.

- We should now have artwork as on the image below.

- Some of the template objects are starting to disappear, buried below actual cover images. More on this later.

Chapter 7 – Back Cover Elements

We are nearing the end of the task of composing the artwork. The design of the back cover can be very flexible. You can let your imagination dictate what you want to convey, however there are elements that it typically contains. They are exemplified below.

Instructions for this section have been simplified since by now we should know how to manipulate text, color blocks, and images.

The design of the elements for the spine of the book, a simple task by now, have also been included in this section

Back Cover and Spine Blocks

- It is assumed that by now we know how to place colored rectangle blocks with no visible edges and then fill those with text, or overlay them with pictures.
- It is time to complete the back cover page.
- We will place several elements on the back cover:
    - a solid background color rectangle that covers the whole back cover, with color compatible with the front page artwork
    - a few teaser lines about the book, at the top
    - the book title, optionally including a secondary title, near the center
    - a section containing a few words about the author
    - an author photograph
    - the required 2"x1.2" white block which CreateSpace will eventually fill with a UPC product code

- We will also add two text blocks, rotated to vertical, on the spine of the book.
  - title at the top
  - author name at the bottom
  - CreateSpace requires these for books thicker than 101 pages; thinner books should have no spine text.
- We now have the front and back cover artwork as follows:

- For better visual appearance, blocks should be properly aligned relative to each other.
- The title and author blocks on the front cover are already pre-aligned by virtue of having placed centered text within blocks that were already aligned to each other (aligned to the spine).
- Text blocks on the spine can be aligned along their center line by using the submenu that shows up under *Arrange* within the *Drawing* tools in PowerPoint.
- The text blocks in the back cover can be aligned to each other's left edge using the same tool menu described above.

- Alternatively, a thin vertical line could be drawn in the workspace and be dragged to a desired location. Art blocks can be aligned by snapping them to that line. Delete the line when done.

- We should leave a small border between text blocks and the edges of the cover. A space of 0.25" is sufficient. We do not need to use a template for this... just inset the text visually as you would visualize the page.

- What happened to the template elements that we used? They are in the composed imagery, but buried beneath the components that we can see, since those were successively added on top of the template material. The only visible remnant (if you look carefully at the above image) of the template is the center line in the spine of the book. This is because it was drawn longer than the height of the spine.

- If at this time you can see elements of the template besides the vertical line noted above, it is because somehow they have managed to surface above the image elements that should be in the foreground. If that is the case then each visible template element must be sent back below the cover art components. This can be done by selecting the object we wish to move and using the *Order Object* within the *Arrange* menu showing up in the tool ribbon at the top of PowerPoint's *Home* menu.

- The background template objects must be removed before we export the document for submittal for publication. This is covered in the next chapter.

- The following two images show what the submitted cover art looks like as seen through the CreateSpace Digital proofer.

- You can see that the dashed lines identifying the spine of the book are precisely on the spine portion of the composed artwork, as we expected.

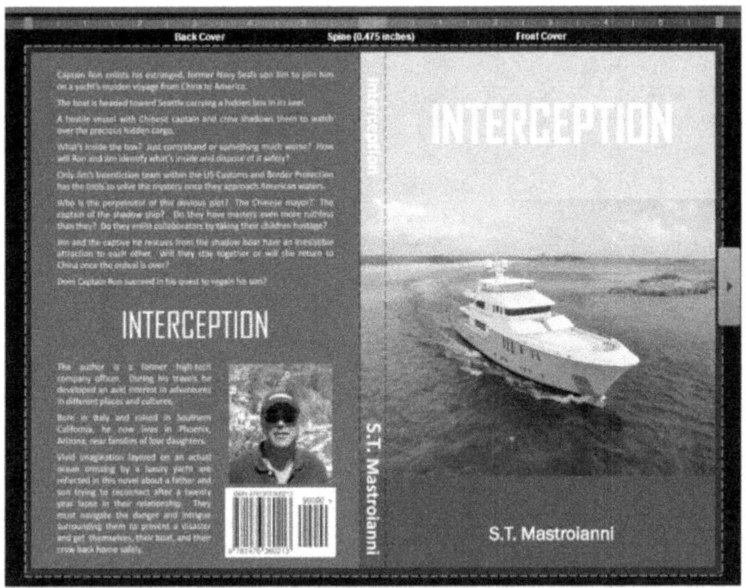

Cover art example, as seen on CreateSpace Digital Proofer

Cover art example, as seen on CreateSpace rotatable 3D view

Chapter 8 – Removing The Template

We wish to upload to CreateSpace only the cover art with no hidden template elements embedded. This is to prevent unwanted objects in the visible art, objects that might pop up while CreateSpace "flattens" (removes any object layering information) the data.

Removing Template from Composite Art
- The template material must be removed before saving the composite artwork to a PDF file.
- One way to do this is to insert an additional blank slide into the PowerPoint worksheet and transfer onto that only the desired artwork. This page is what will then be used to create the PDF file for submittal.
- This approach is much easier and much less error prone than the alternative which would be to select all the background template objects and to delete them. This is because the template material is hidden below live images and may be hard to see, select, and delete.
- Navigate to the original slide that contains the artwork and template material underneath it. Holding down on the *Shift* key, select all the elements of the cover art that we wish to export to the PDF file by left clicking on them one at a time.
  - front cover picture
  - front cover title block
  - front cover author block
  - spine title block

- o   spine author block
- o   spine filler rectangles above and below picture
- o   back cover color block
- o   back cover teaser text
- o   back cover book title
- o   back cover author text
- o   back cover author picture
- o   UPC place holder block (recall this can be anywhere on the back cover; as long as it is of the right dimension and white in color then CreateSpace will find it)
- *Copy* all these elements (all at once since you additively selected them using the *Shift click* method).
- Navigate to the blank slide and *Paste* them there.
- The resulting image is the final composite artwork that we will soon save as a high resolution PDF file.
- Copying and pasting all elements at once is the quickest way to get the job done, however two problems may arise:
    - o   some people may have difficulty keeping track of which objects were clicked and which were not, or may have difficulty with selected objects moving while clicking each additional one on the list
    - o   when pasting all the objects at once onto the new worksheet, some positions may be shifted
    - o   shifting occurs because the software may not be able to keep track of exactly how each element was positioned relative to a neighbor
    - o   you can see the shifting effect by alternatively viewing the old page and the new page by using the Page Up and the Page Down keys on the keyboard
- If either of the above problems shows up, then patiently select, copy, and past one object at a time and watch your new composite page build up one item at a time.

- It should be obvious that we are addressing a limitation of PowerPoint. Software dedicated to graphics manipulation will have layering capability by which the template could be on one layer, and the actual artwork on another. Layers can then be selected at will. PowerPoint does not have this layering capability.

Chapter 9 – Configuring PDF Export

CreateSpace does not accept cover art as a PowerPoint document. It only accepts a single PDF (Portable Document Format) page containing the composite cover art.

PowerPoint can export its file content to a PDF format but to preserve high resolution images some configuration modifications need to be made.

PowerPoint as installed is configured to export a resolution of only 96dpi. Regardless of the quality of the original artwork, this is what will be saved as a PDF file if PowerPoint's configuration attributes are not changed.

The value of 96dpi is a carryover from display screens at a time when the technology was only capable of this number of dots per inch. It appears that PowerPoint was, and still is, primarily intended to be used with displays. This low resolution is not acceptable for cover art. This quality is well below the minimum 200dpi that we established as a minimum for success.

PowerPoint must be configured to export its data to a PDF document at 300dpi resolution.

Configuring PowerPoint to export a PDF page at 300dpi:

- This configuration procedure involves adding a Windows registry key as explained in the Microsoft support page found at this web address:
  https://support.microsoft.com/en-us/help/827745/how-to-change-the-export-resolution-of-a-powerpoint-slide

- The Microsoft support page addresses PowerPoint versions 2003, 2007, 2010, 2013, and 2016.

- NOTE: be very careful when making Windows registry changes. Make sure that you only select and change the items indicated below. Changes to other line items can cause software functionality issues.

- The procedure is explained below as it applies to a PC computer running the Win10 (Windows 10) operating system and Office 2007. Other Windows and Office versions have the same capabilities but menus may look slightly different.

- This will be the "trickiest part" of what must be done to use PowerPoint to generate high resolution PDF images, but do not let it intimidate you. Clear instructions will show you what to do.

- In the lower left hand corner of your screen find the *Type here to search* window, the box with the magnifying glass icon. This is right next to the *START* menu (the window icon) on your PC screen.

- Type in *run.*

- A menu will pop up. Select the icon named *Run Desktop app.*

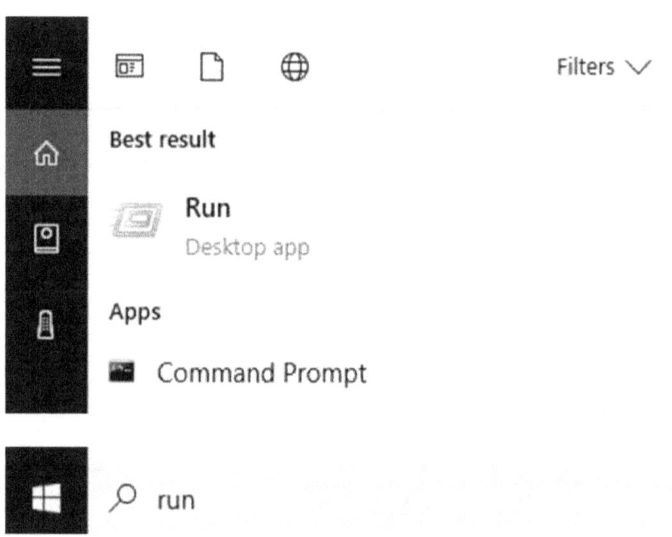

- If you are using earlier versions of Windows, the *Run* command can be found by clicking the lower left hand *START* icon and then clicking on *Run* from the list of programs that shows up in the popup window. The remainder of the instructions will be identical.

- Type in *regedit* in the window that pops up after selecting *Run*.

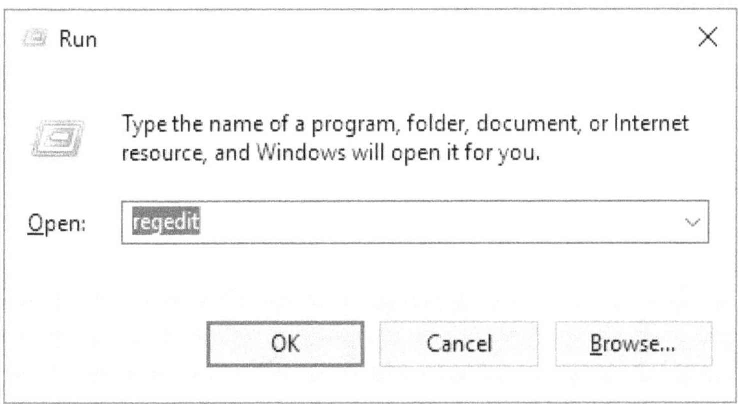

- Select *OK*. The following window will pop up. Notice that the symbol to the left of the line *HKEY_CURRENT_USER* had to be clicked to expand the list (symbol now points downward instead of to the right).

- Similarly the symbol to the left of *Software* had to be clicked to expand the list contained in that block.

- Similarly, the symbol to the left of *Microsoft* had to be clicked to expand that list.

- For now, pay no attention to the information that shows up in the right hand pane of the window.

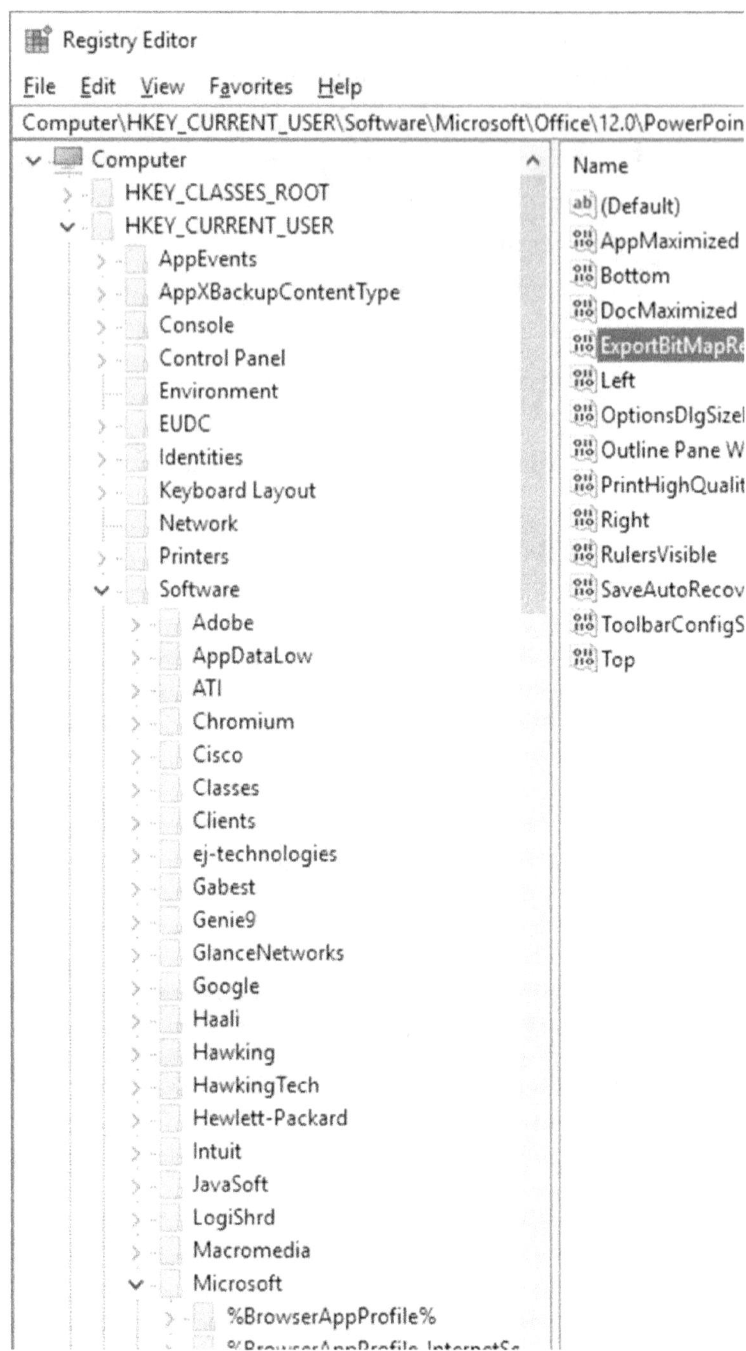

- Within the block *Microsoft*, scroll down to find *Office*, then *12.0*, and then down to *PowerPoint*. Notice that the symbol to the left of line entries must be clicked to expand the lists. The number *12.0* corresponds to Office 2007 (on my computer). A higher number may show up on your computer if you have a newer version of Office. Select the highest number that shows up on the *Registry Editor*.

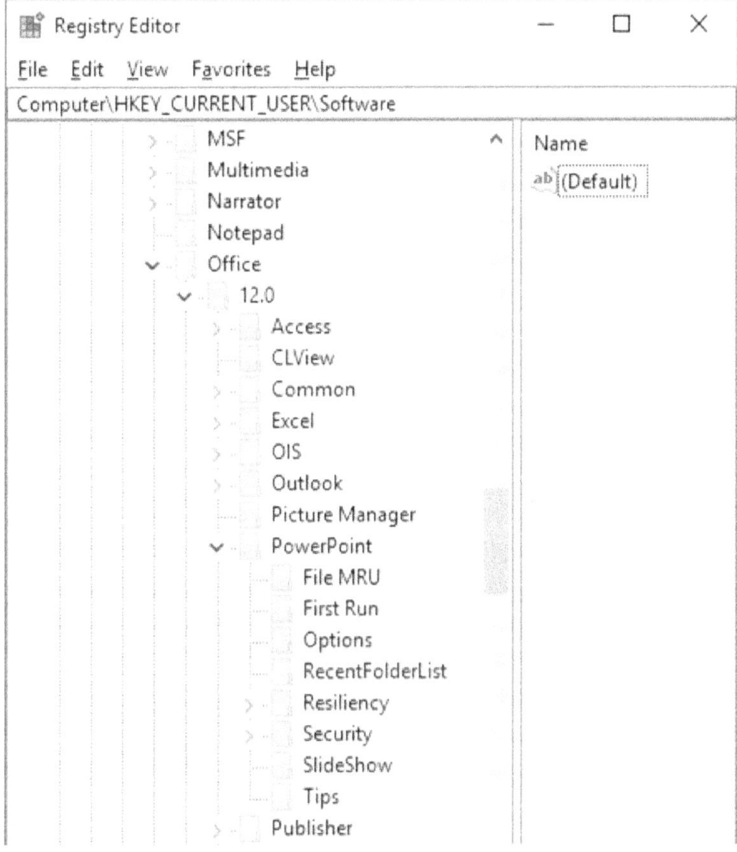

- Move cursor over the word *Options* under the *PowerPoint* block. The panel on the right will now show data in which we are interested.

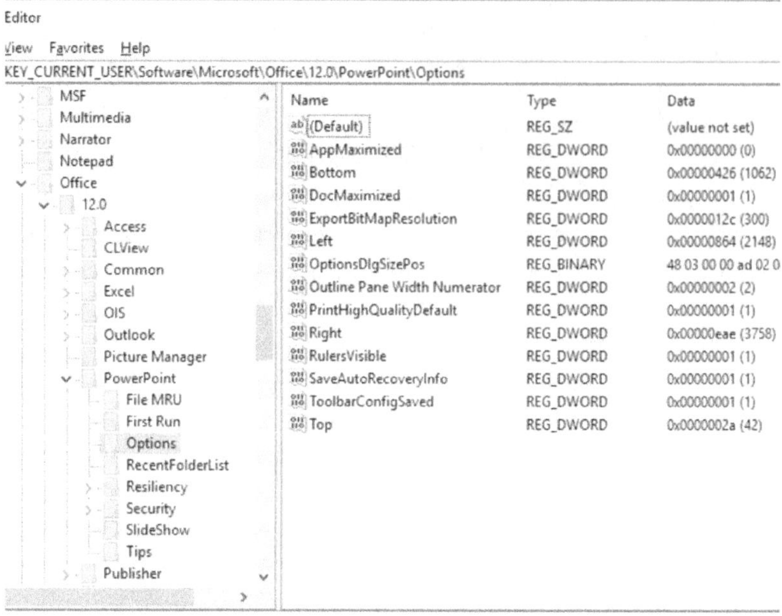

- Look carefully in the right hand pane where you can see the line entry *ExportBitMapResolution*. You can see two fields to the right of *ExportBitMapResolution*. The first shows *REG_DWORD* and the second shows *0x0000012c (300)*.

- *REG_DWORD* means registry double wide word, and the value *0x0000012c* is the hexadecimal value for 300, which is shown in normal decimal notation in parentheses *(300)*.

- The entire line *ExportBitMapResolution* in the right hand pane shows up in the above image because it was placed in the system on my computer. This is the registry entry that needs to be added to set the export resolution of PowerPoint to 300dpi.

- Unless someone has already done this work on your PC, that line will be missing and you will see an image showing the right hand pane as shown below. The list of elements may be different. That's alright, but the line *ExportBitMapResolution* should not be there because it has not yet been created.

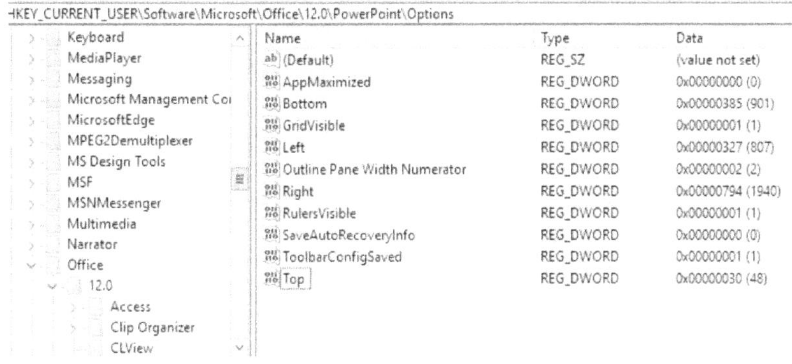

- The line *ExportBitMapResolution* must be inserted into the registry on your computer.

- With the mouse cursor on a blank spot on the right hand pane, click the right mouse button.

- A popup menu *New* will show up.

- Hover the cursor over the word *New* and a second popup menu will give you choices to select.

- Select *DWORD (32-bit) value*.

- Notice that an additional line named *NewValue#1* has been added to the registry (the bottom line in right panel).

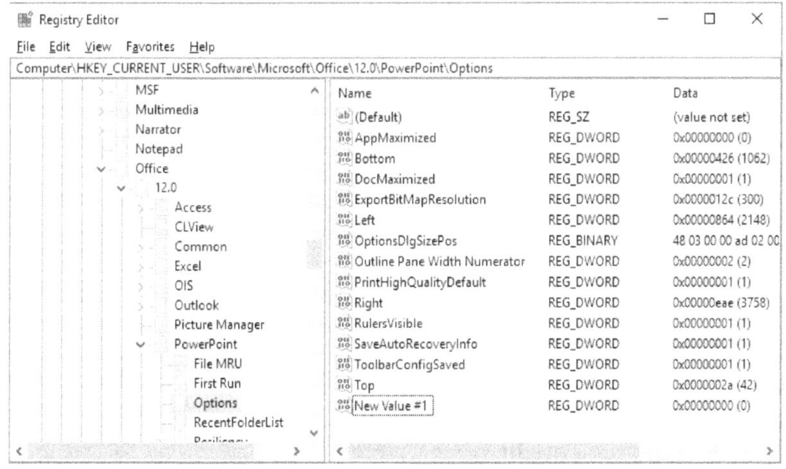

- Hover the mouse over the words *NewValue#1* and left click to select. While the word is highlighted, right click and a new popup menu with choices will show up. Select *Rename*.

- Type in the new name for this line entry. This must be entered exactly, one single word with no misspelling: *ExportBitMapResolution*.

- Right click on the new name *ExportBitMapResolution* and a new popup window will show up with choices. *Select Modify Binary Data...* You will see the popup below.

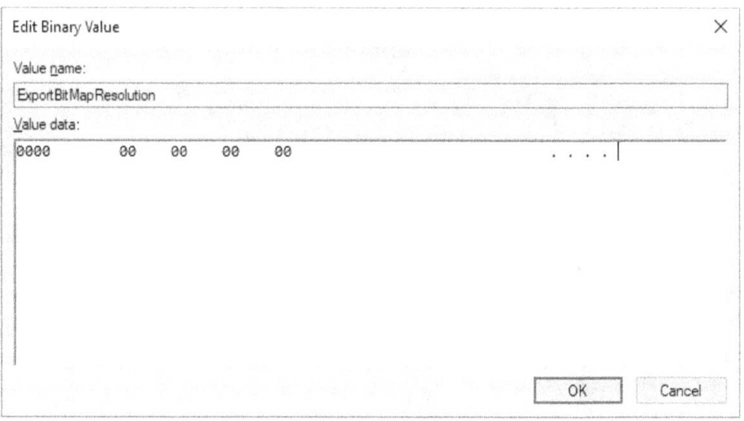

- Select the first group of two zeros. When they show up highlighted, overtype with the new value, *2C*.

- Select the second group of two zeros. Overtype with the value *01*. Press OK.

- It was shown earlier that we wish to enter the value 300 (to specify 300dpi) which in computer hexadecimal format corresponds to 12C. So, why are typing in values 'backwards'?

- Hexadecimal numbers must be entered two digits at a time, with the least significant digits first and most significant digits last (essentially right to left).

- That is why we input the value *2C* first, followed by the value 1 (actually *01* which includes a leading 0 as a filler digit).

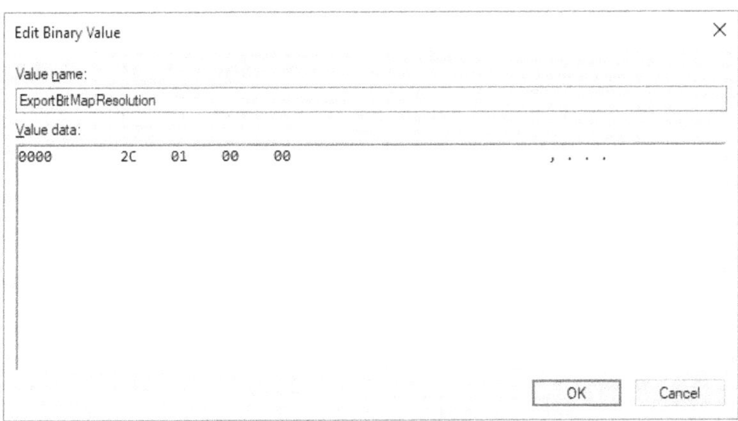

- The value was entered, hexadecimal number (01) (2C).
- Select OK.

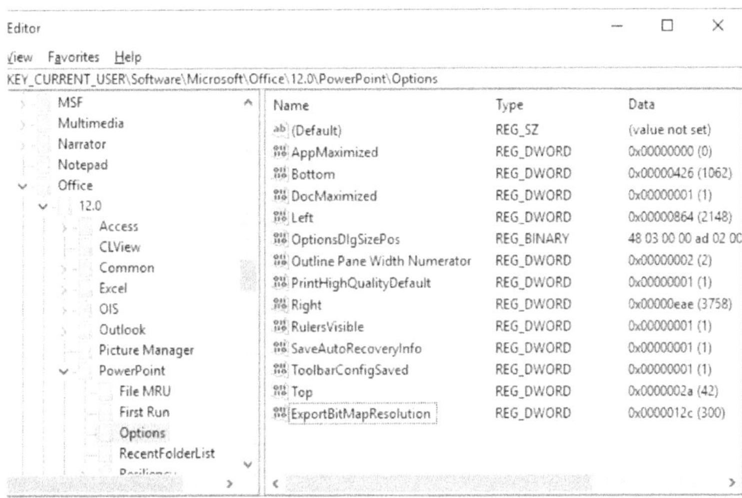

- Notice the new registry line added, *ExportBitMapResolution*. In the far right hand field notice the value, *12c* in hexadecimal notation, and in parentheses the value of *300* in normal decimal notation. Upper case or lower case has no significance in this context.

- Congratulations! We are done! When you exit the box by clicking on the X in the upper right hand corner, you will have saved a new Windows registry key that instructs PowerPoint to export files at 300 dots per inch resolution, as required by CreateSpace and other publishing platforms. This registry modification will remain in effect on the computer on which it was installed, and will be applied to all future PowerPoint documents.

Chapter 10 – Saving Final File As PDF

An important fact is that the final product, the PDF document to be submitted for the cover art, must be generated from one single PowerPoint slide. A multiple-page PDF document will be rejected.

It is also important to understand what is meant by 'flat data', imagery in which all the layered components have been combined. Since we composed the artwork using layered elements, this would appear to be a problem.

Data must be flattened somewhere along the way before it can be printed. You must do this, unless by default you push the problem down the line and let CreateSpace or your other chosen publisher do it for you. CreateSpace will flag this, but their verification process fixes this issue with little effort.

CreateSpace suggests saving data as a PDF/X instead of the familiar PDF format. A similar version of this is PDF/A. The latter is available on most Microsoft Office platforms.

The advantages of the X or the A versions is that they reduce the content to the simplest format, suitable for archiving into the next century because they remove enhancements that may not be propagated forward. This includes transparency and layering.

This author recommends using the standard PDF format. The reason is that if you used transparent images, for example the book title in a transparent block so that you can see part of the underlying photo, then the archival PDF's will remove the transparency and you will not see the underlying image. The differing results between PDF and PDF/A are shown in figures later in this section.

Saving Final Artwork as Single-Page PDF File

- CreateSpace only accepts composite artwork on a single page.
- The PowerPoint workspace now contains two slides.
- We will soon select the slide that has the cover art only (no template material) and save it as a single PDF page.
- CreateSpace <u>prefers</u> to receive 'flat data'. This means that the artwork should not contain layered elements.
- Clearly, our PowerPoint workspace contains blocks that we have laid on top of each other.
- The function of exporting such layered data to standard PDF format still preserves layering information… data is not flattened, even when exporting to PDF.
- Some PowerPoint versions have facility to flatten data prior to saving as PDF. Newer versions do, but mine, part of Office 2007, does not. If you also have this limitation, it is not a catastrophic shortcoming, as addressed below.
- Submitting un-flattened data to CreateSpace seems to cause no real issue. They will return a flag stating that the imagery contains layering, but the flag also states that they have repaired it. Repaired, that is, by them flattening the data. In the final result, this small flaw causes no problem.
- Navigate to the PowerPoint slide that has no template material within it. In the example we have used so far, I look for the absence of the center line through the spine.
- Click on the icon at the very upper left hand corner of the PowerPoint window and select *SaveAs*.
- In the popup window, select *PDF or XPS*.
- In the menu that popped up, note that the *File name* is pre-filled in with the current file name. This means that both the PowerPoint file and the soon to be saved PDF file will have the same name unless you change the PDF file name here. Same name is good, for archiving purposes. You can tell

them apart from each other by the different icon that will be associated with the file.

- Check to see that the *Save as type* box is preloaded with *PDF*, otherwise select *PDF* from the pull down menu.

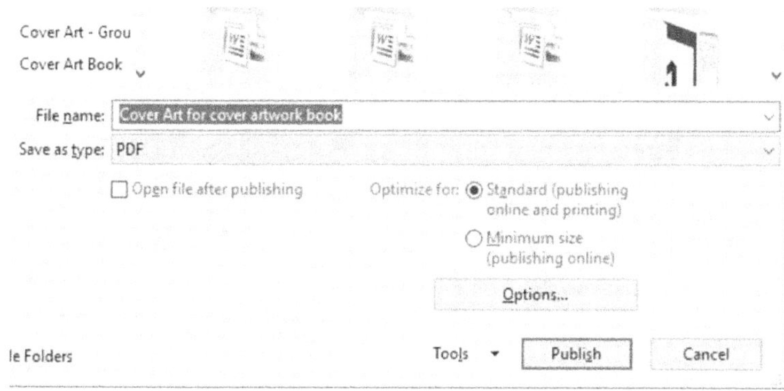

- Click on the *Options* box. You will see the popup window shown below.

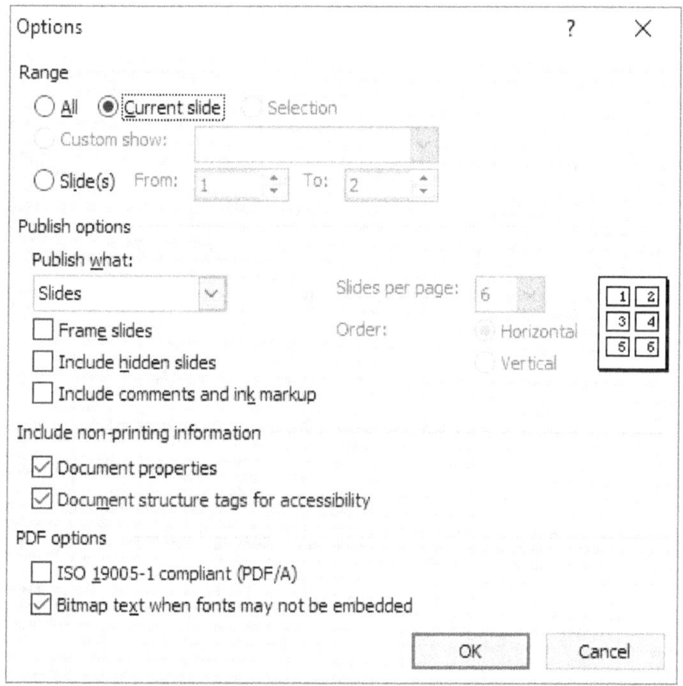

- Select *Current Slide*. This insures that only a single page is saved.
- Click *OK*.
- You are back to the *Save As* menu. Click *Publish*.
- A PDF file of the single slide you selected has now appeared in the same folder where the PowerPoint artwork file resides.
- Open the file and inspect it carefully. It should not look any different than the PowerPoint slide version that you saw earlier.
- WE ARE DONE. This is the PDF you want to submit to CreateSpace.

**Cover Art for cover
artwork book.pdf**

- If after submittal you still get a flag stating that some images are not high enough resolution, do not be alarmed.
- It may be that while composing our artwork some of the imagery has dropped slightly below 200dpi due to minor sizing or adjustment that we have done. "Slightly below" 200dpi will not cause any discernible image blurring.
- In the example we have just finished, there was an element that generated such a flag for low resolution. CreateSpace does not tell you which element.
- My own analysis identified the author photograph as the culprit. Because it was severely cropped from a much larger picture, it ended up being a few pixels short of 200dpi to cause the flag to be thrown. No harm done…. The rest of the imagery is clear and sharp, and on the CreateSpace printed copy the author photograph also had no noticeable blur.

Chapter 11 – Creating This Book's Cover

It seemed an obvious thought to apply the methodology outlined in this book to actually make the book cover for this very same book.

It also seemed logical that a book about making book covers should allude to book covers on its own front cover.

It took only a few minutes to bring down a few volumes from my library and arrange them on a sunlit living room carpet in order to take a high resolution picture with my trusty Canon full-frame camera.

I decided to adapt the format we created, with some simple changes.

I wanted the photograph to cover the entire front cover. This made it necessary then to change the Title and Author text block from solid rectangles to transparent rectangles. Transparency was selected at 30%, allowing enough photo detail to show through but still allowing enough contrast to clearly show the text in the blocks.

Recall that transparency is not preserved if saving as PDF/X or PDF/A. Currently, submitting a standard PDF document does, as was explained earlier.

A quick update of the 'teaser' lines and author info on the back page and colorizing the placeholder rectangles to a brown/tan theme and the job was complete. It took less than one hour to do the entire job, thanks to the preparation work that went into the cover art example.

The new cover as seen on a PDF page is shown below. It is identically the cover of this book.

File saved as PDF/A – not submitted!

File saved as standard PDF format and as used for this book

- Transparency was preserved in the PDF file, as visible on the title and author text blocks, but not in the PDF/A format.

- Note the lack of spine text in both files. This book contains less than 101 pages and therefore has no room for such text blocks, so none must be included as specified by CreateSpace.

Chapter 12 – Final Thoughts

The information presented in this book should be sufficient to allow the mechanical creation of book cover art that will satisfy the needs to self-publish on platforms like CreateSpace.

Such cover art can be produced with the simplest of tools, PowerPoint, presumed to be available to almost anyone that has ever had to prepare any presentation material.

PowerPoint comes with Microsoft Office as does the text editor Word. Any author that uses Word to write the book's interior text file should have access to PowerPoint.

It should be evident then that the approach used makes it possible for an author to create cover art at absolutely no incremental cost other than his/her own time and effort.

The one item that generates the most appeal, or lack thereof, for a book cover is the front page art. This is what gets prominently displayed as an icon in a book seller's web site such as Amazon.

The example cover generated in this book is still a pretty simple piece of art. It relies for its appeal on a single photograph which occupies the central space of the front cover.

A quick search for images of commercial book covers (for example, searching for "book covers" on Google Images) reveals a large variety in the appearance of commercially created cover art.

Some commercial art uses a single photograph overlaid with text, much as the example in this book. Other books have an image created by an artist, a drawing conveying conceptual images of the book's thematic messages. Other books just have fancy textual information.

CREATING ARTWORK FOR BOOK COVERS

There are several points to be made after comparing the example in this book with professionally created covers.

First, recall that the objective here was to "do it yourself" with tools you already have, and using easily obtainable images such as a photograph that can also convey a main theme. In the example, the main thread of the story was a transoceanic adventure on a luxury yacht. A picture of an actual luxury vessel seemed appropriate for the story.

Additionally what has been shown are the key mechanics of how to combine text and images and preserve resolution adequate for publishing. Readers can use the basic tools shown and add their own imagination and resources to the task. Maybe some will have access to conceptual art creations that can be used. Images and text do not have to be the exactly the same number, or located exactly as in the example. They can be manipulated to reflect the individual author's vision.

Below is a summary of key points that were covered in this book. Many involved finding improvements for shortcomings of PowerPoint. The implementation of workarounds is what allowed us to successfully produce book cover art using a PC with only Microsoft's PowerPoint and the free version of Adobe's PDF reader installed.

PowerPoint Procedures for Optimizing Cover Art Resolution:
- Proper PowerPoint worksheet page setup.
- Selecting maximum resolution when saving PowerPoint file.
- Avoiding image compression when saving PowerPoint file.
- Configuring PowerPoint for maximum resolution when exporting to PDF. This involves making a Windows registry change.

"Best Practices" for Improving Appearance of Visual Objects:
- Selecting "Snap Objects to Other Objects".
- Preserving images' aspect ratio when resizing them.

- Defining the size of an object using exact sizing.
- Choosing the PDF type to preserve art objects' transparency.

"Best Practices" to Minimize Errors when Working with PowerPoint:

- Using transparency in template objects.
- Proper scaling of images using pixel counts.

***

Finally I would like to leave the most observant readers with one final challenge (remember, the Chinese define "challenge" as "danger/opportunity").

Recall that we went to great pains to make sure that PowerPoint will export to PDF at a resolution of 300dpi.

We also realized early on that upon the first *Save* of a PowerPoint document, and upon each subsequent *Save*, PowerPoint will limit the resolution of stored images at 220dpi. Although this was deemed to be adequate for printed art, it does not fully utilize the PDF capabilities that we have installed.

Recall also that PowerPoint's image downsizing to 220dpi happens only when performing the *Save* function but not prior to that step. It was mentioned in this book that PowerPoint can hold pictures in their full original resolution, while you are working on a worksheet… until you issue that *Save* command.

Here is the challenge. What if one were to keep all the original photos handy, place them on a PowerPoint worksheet, and when finished composing then *Save As* PDF to generate the submitted art. Notice that the *Save* as PowerPoint has been averted before conversion to PDF, therefore one can render art limited now only by the 300dpi export to PDF capability.

Although the method described above produces the highest resolution (300dpi, assuming that the original pictures meet or exceed this goal), the author does not recommend following this approach.

The reason for discouraging this procedure is simple. Because image resolution would be lost upon that first *Save*, then this process makes archiving of file revisions almost impossible. One would have to remember, or write down somewhere, which pictures were used to create which version of artwork created and submitted.

***

It took this author three passes with three successive books through CreateSpace to finally figure out how to best use the tools at hand. I hope that what I have passed on to you is as helpful a guide as it is for my own use.

Appendix – Scaling Pictures

This section provides additional information on how to scale a picture to any arbitrary aspect ratio. Aspect ratio is the number that results by taking one of the dimensions, such as width, and dividing it by the other dimension, height. This parameter is needed in order to fit an image exactly into the space held by a placeholder rectangle that was positioned in the artwork. The aspect ratio of the image must match the aspect ratio of the placeholder rectangle.

The most detailed unit of measure for dimensions of a photograph is the pixel. Photos are measured in units of pixels for width and for height.

The most basic tool that provides picture editing / cropping capabilities using pixel counts is *Microsoft Office Picture Manager* that comes with versions of *Microsoft Office*.

The task at hand then is to figure out the aspect ratio of the placeholder rectangle and then scale the picture, using pixels, to provide exactly the same aspect ratio.

The picture can then be inserted into the available space by sizing it using one of the handles at the corners (in this way preserving aspect ratio), and snapping it into place. If properly dimensioned during the scaling process, the picture should fill the space exactly.

As an example we will use the photograph that was chosen for the cover art for this book and show how it was scaled to fit exactly on the space reserved for the front cover. Recall that we placed a rectangle of exactly this size on our cover art template.

- In the case selected, we wish to cover the page entirely, so the edited photo will need to look something like a portrait mode photo:
    - height of image = height of page + bottom "bleed" area + top "bleed" area
    - **height** of image = 9" + 0.125" + 0.125" = **9.25"**
    - width of image = width of page + right "bleed" area
    - **width** of image = 6" + 0.125" = **6.125"**
    - aspect ratio = Height / Width
    - **aspect ratio** = 9.25" / 6.125" = **1.510**
- The source picture intended as the central element of the front cover is shown below.

- We do a quick pixel size check by opening the picture:
    - right click on the image
    - select *Open With* from the popup menu
    - Select *Microsoft Office Picture Manager* from the popup menu. If this item does not show up on your computer, you will have to find some other application that allows photo editing using pixel count. The latest Microsoft picture tool that installs with WIN10, something called *Photos*, does not appear to have this capability.
    - select *Edit Pictures* from the topmost tool ribbon

- o at this point, if you hover the cursor over the image on the screen you will be able to see the pixel count
  - o for the picture above, the numbers displayed are 4145 x 3094 for width and height respectively
  - o this is a landscape formatted photo, with the width larger than the height
- We want to extract a useful image in a portrait format to fit our book cover.
- We will preserve all the height and only scale (crop) in the width dimension.
- Using the aspect ratio calculated earlier, 1.510, we can calculate how many pixels we can have in the new width dimension assuming we preserve the entire height of the photo:
  - o width in pixels = height in pixels / aspect ratio
  - o width in pixels = 3094 / 1.510 = 2049
- Number of pixels in the width dimension that we wish to crop out is the number of the width of the current picture minus the number that we wish to retain.
- Number of width pixels to be cropped:
  - o 4145 – 2049 = 2096
  - o we will allocate some of the pixels to the left edge, and the remainder to the right edge of the photo
  - o select *Crop* from the right menu panel within the picture viewer
  - o a popup menu shows fields labeled *Left*, *Right*, *Top*, *Bottom*; counts of pixels to be cropped can be inputted here
  - o enter the value 1000 in the *Left* box, and the remainder, 2096 – 1000 = 1096, in the *Right* box
  - o press *OK* and the picture will be cropped, appearing now as a portrait mode picture
  - o save the new cropped picture

- Re-Open (to make sure you are viewing the new image) the cropped picture with *Microsoft Office Picture Manager.*

- Hover the mouse over the image. You should now see its new dimensions as 2049 x 3094 pixels, as we expected.

- This picture can now be copied and pasted onto the cover art worksheet. Size it using one corner handle such that you can snap one corner of it to the where it belongs on the template. Use the other corner handle now to size it and snap it to the other corner.

- By definition, if we have done the arithmetic correctly, this image will fit exactly into the space reserved for the front cover of our book.

- The resulting image is shown below. It is identically what was used for the front cover of this book.

Picture scaled correctly for front cover using pixel counts

NOTES